rue

rue

poems

melissa bull

ANVIL PRESS » VANCOUVER

Copyright © 2015 by Melissa Bull

All rights reserved. No part of this book may be reproduced by any means without the prior written permission of the publisher, with the exception of brief passages in reviews. Any request for photocopying or other reprographic copying of any part of this book must be directed in writing to access: The Canadian Copyright Licensing Agency, One Yonge Street, Suite 800, Toronto, Ontario, Canada, M5E 1E5.

Anvil Press Publishers Inc.
P.O. Box 3008, Main Post Office
Vancouver, B.C. V6B 3X5 CANADA
www.anvilpress.com

Library and Archives Canada Cataloguing in Publication

Bull, Melissa, 1977-, author
    Rue / Melissa Bull.

Poems.
ISBN 978-1-77214-016-3 (pbk.)

    I. Title.

PS8603.U538R84 2015   C811'.6   C2015-901619-3

Printed and bound in Canada
Cover illustration by Lasse Mathiesen Køhlert
Interior by HeimatHouse
Represented in Canada by the Publishers Group Canada
Distributed by Raincoast Books

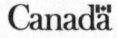

The publisher gratefully acknowledges the financial assistance of the Canada Council for the Arts, the Canada Book Fund, and the Province of British Columbia through the B.C. Arts Council and the Book Publishing Tax Credit.

*For my mother, Suzanne, who showed me
"how to look among the garbage and the flowers."*

"Primrose like something prim, the way a smudge
of colour is as good as it will get.
The way one hands out rue like sunscreen
cuz it's going to be one of those Sundays."

— David McGimpsey

"Now I am quietly waiting for
the catastrophe of my personality
to seem beautiful again."

— Frank O'Hara

TABLE OF CONTENTS

BROOD

Bleeding Hearts / 13
Claremont, Apt. 45 / 17
Fever in Gaspé / 21
Vaillant / 23
Cours du samedi / 25
Zabriskie Point / 26
The Stare / 27
Flanks Sounding Heavily with Expiration / 29
Edisto / 30
Rivière-du-Loup / 31
Mount Cannon by Way of Lonesome Lake / 32

SKIRTING PETITE-PATRIE

Down with a Case of WTF / 37
La Calera / 38
Nevsky Prospekt / 41
Neva / 42
Scaffolding / 43
Recipe / 47
Callow and Rue / 48
Near Miss / 50
Neuter / 51
Jean-Talon / 53
Dante / 54
Everett / 55
d'Ici / 56
Arc / 57

Tithes / 58
Valentine / 60
Game / 61
The Lark / 63
Four Eyes / 64
Plaza Saint-Hubert Reconciliation Number
  Double-Digit / 66
Draft / 67
Radii / 68
Call Me Klaus / 69
Flush / 70
Wont / 71
Ruse / 73
That Line / 76
Not a Good Time / 77

ELOQUENT AREAS

Fuse / 81
Weather / 82
Two Pears / 84
The Heart of an Ox / 85
The Grief Marathon / 89
Now / 91
BATTERMEDOWN! / 93
Mourning? / 95
1:00 - 2:00 PM Décarie and Paré / 96
Sainte-Catherine / 100
These / 101

Acknowledgements / 103

BROOD

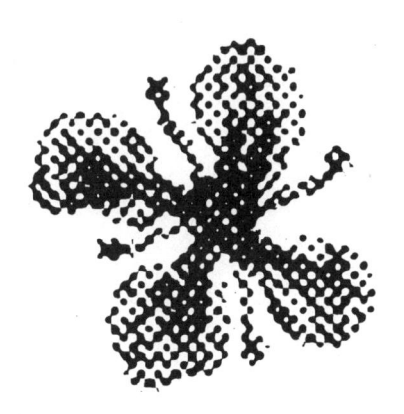

Bleeding Hearts

i.

It was the leftover mustard. The mustard-coloured mustard smeared my father's upperlip and auburn 'stache from another smoked meatskin sandwich he'd picked up after his nightshift.

At first my mother would wait up for him. There were years when waiting up and wiping mustard from his mouth was still acceptable. When someone said to her, at the Press Club, *You're with The Bull! He's such a slob!* she'd still been indignant, she hadn't started thinking that talking to him was like communicating with a mattress.

Her favourite song was still "Angie" even though it didn't make her cry anymore now she didn't have to take the commuter train from Roxboro to Dorval to teach art to disaffected suburban teens.

ii.

Around the time my parents met, my mother had tried and failed to tame a skunk. My father recalls visiting my mother at her apartment on Old Orchard, the way her skunk

>(*sa moufette*, her muffette)

>>chased her around the
kitchen, biting at her heels.

I picture rodent teeth, squirrel teeth. She'd had its stink sack pouch whatever it's called removed, or maybe the skunk came with it cut out, whatever had happened, it wasn't supposed to spray, but it did, somehow, a less toxic odour, but still pongish, ripe, pissy.

It was maybe third in a line of pets

> Twenty? More? Cats, dogs, gerbils, rabbits, birds—

> my mother would get rid of.

Certainly some of them were dumped for pissing in the wrong places. Maybe a third of them.

iii.

Everywhere she lives, my mother loads her yard up with:

bleeding hearts
lilacs
rhododendrons
raspberry bushes
sumac
currants

iv.

My mother shot pictures
            —a giant, overexposed thumb—

                she caught her brood of
            molasses-cookie dark

moody-faced adolescents, when they took the train from Roxboro to NDG, smoking Gitanes, eating apricots on Mount Royal, stuffing fistfuls of autumn leaves down their snap-plaid shirts. Or pics of Joey Smallwood speaking to a crowd of pre-health-care Newfoundlanders looking like a scene out of a Hieronymus Bosch triptych

                —the goitres, the town idiots—
                    in a village called
                    Virgin's Tickle.

My mother's got a shotgun in her closet. She won't have it registered. She hangs on to it to remember the one time she used it to shoot ducks, when she was a teenager somewhere in Mauricie.

Whenever she talks about tacking ducks, I remember that scene from *Out of Africa* before Karen Blixen/Meryl Streep gets hitched to her syphilis bad boy and she's looking regal and shooting at birds.

Maybe pheasants.

vi.

She wanted an English baby. A family do-over. A fresh start. She wanted to make my father a baby, she said, because he had kind eyes.

    (A multitude of ladyfriend psychiatric patients would echo.)

vii.

Papa won a contest at Canadian Press

    —an all-expenses trip to Ireland for two.

He said in Ireland my mother would drink pints of Guinness while he had half-pints of Harp.

She got into a fight at a bed and breakfast, remembering only a feeling of shame in the morning, a sense they had to switch rooming houses

    —there's a picture of them in four-poster bed in a
        castle, their messy heads poking
    out from under a quilt, their faces mischievous—

I was born the next year.

Claremont, Apt. 45

I wake up in a narrow room. My mouth feels dirty. I wipe my teeth on my topsheet. I get up. Suzanne pours me a bowl of Cheerios. I add a teaspoon of white sugar. I like the concave metallic of the teaspoon inside my mouth. Suzanne tells me not to bite the cutlery. Our black and white cat Tom howls for the breakfast he's already had then jumps to the top of the door and watches us from his narrow ledge. It's a double-hinged door; it opens either way like the doors of a saloon. He moans. Suzanne yells at him, *Christophecolomb!* He jumps, she gives him a kick toward the living room.

Suzanne sits at the edge of a yellow lacquered table she found in the garbage, smoking a du Maurier in her nightgown, her hair sleepflat, or washeddamp, coffee in a ceramic mug circa 1973, from the Old Orchard Street apartment from the year before my father. That Suzanne is beautiful is a thought that plays on repeat. I eat my Cheerios with a teaspoonful of sugar. She runs herself a bath in the old clawfoot tub. The bathroom is hung with wallpaper she invented—series of *Gazette* comic strips dating back from years of paper collections. I read Andy Cap every time I take a crap. It's all very pop art, very 1986. Outside the bathroom, mannequins are trapped upsidedown in cement bloodslabs, papiermaché bellies exploding Barbie knots. I eat my Cheerios. Bring the bowl to my mouth to drink the sweetened, roomwarmed milk. The spoon on the table leaves a white puddle I stick my finger into and spread thin.

At night we eat shepherd's pie. At night we eat pasta with butter and pepper and salt. We eat frozen corn and feel the cold kernels burst in our mouths. The taste is unappealing but the squish is amazing. We do it again and again. Coldcorn coldsquish. In winter's early nights we eat early. My pink backpack slumped on the floor by the door to my room, homework to be done for the next day, word games I'm eager to play. My swimming suit to wash. The white stripes are getting seethrough but we don't have enough money for another yet. The low porcelain sink, the slipping tiles. The overheated apartment. Suzanne, animated, porcelain bracelet hanging off her left chinawhite arm. Onions frying.

The sound, the perpetual sound of pigeons cooing and feathering and winging along the ridges of our windows.

Suzanne in black heels that strap around her ankles, black satin pants at Christmas, laughing drunkloud, overcharming overdrunk, the smell of perfume and Gitanes and olives and things stewing in rosemary. Pigfoot stew stewing, ragooing. Suzanne is the most beautiful, more beautiful than her daughters or her sons' wives or her friends. They are drunkloud and laughing and in heels and buttoned shirts and laughing and smoking Gitanes.

The sound of the bathwater running. The smell of coffee, of one multigrain toast. The sound of the bathwater, the smell of the toast, Suzanne at her chair with a cigarette, my bedroom door opening but never latching right, pigeons not Vs, pigeons lateral overlapping flocks, soft dinosaur architecture of slums on sills.

Dust gathers under books under socks.

The sound of the bath running. The coffee dripping, the toaster popping the one piece of multigrain bread for Suzanne. She used to be heavier but now she's disciplined herself to this one piece of toast. The sound of Suzanne's alarm clock. Suzanne's alarm clock with the classical station and that calm international French announcer's voice. The lace curtain of her window billowing. The window is open because it's winter and the apartment is overheated. She used to weigh one hundred and ten pounds.

The throwrugs sliding on the tiled floors. The cat meowing as if we haven't fed him, but we have. He sits on the windowledge watching the temptations of chubby pigeons coo neckwalk featurehump rustle and fight out their chromatically aging greys.

Scissors snipping, the whirring sewing machine, cloth speeding under needle. Suzanne knitting with large wooden needles. Butter on the pasta and just a little pepper. The sound of the bath running the sound of the bath running, the water getting too high. Above the shower a plastic heart, neon pink. The sound of the water, the sound of the washing machine hooked up to the sink. Saturday loads of laundry piled over the kitchen floor. Suzanne smoking a cigarette at a family party, body poised into triangles—crossed leg triangles, smoking hand in front of face triangles. Every Slavic feature polished, skin the colour of milkglass. Suzanne crying in her room with bottles of sherry. Suzanne crying in my arms. I can't get my arms around her right. The sound of the pink gingerale fizzing on the coffee table.

I play the piano and tape myself. The brass pedals under my feet. That relief of mute, that relief of pressing, that relief of stretching the echo into legato.

At night, the moon hangs over the fire escape. The pigeons cooing and winging and feathering and struggling for ledge dominance. The sheer polyester curtain hangs over the window, over the radiator. I watch the moon and read on the windowledge. I taperecord Suzanne crying. Gutsobbing with the sherry. Emu. Nine dollars at the SAQ on Victoria. Or the dépanneur. At the dépanneur. At the dépanneur for cigarettes and chocolate bars, a hibiscus, a box of Cheerios.

Dusting each key of the piano's chromatic dust. Thirteen steps, forty-fifth apartment, rent due the first of the month.

She never washes her face before going to bed and every morning her mascara crumbles over her cheeks. I find it unseemly. She farts two farts in the bathroom, standing up. The first is shorter and higher-pitched. I say, *Ouaachhhe* and she says, *Tu préférerais que je pète dans la cuisine?* She puts coffee into the machine. She lights a cigarette. She stands over the sink and says, *Viens, on faire la vaisselle vite vite avant que tu t'en ailles à l'école.*

Fever in Gaspé

A press trip to Percé
with my father and his girlfriend.

I got locked in the car when I was
too sick to tag along
window open just a crack
      —like for a puppy—
I was sixteen.
Fifteen.

Her delighted vindication
as she shut the door
of her red Accord on me.

Allergic to mussels
I'd puked chowder all night
in the B&B's powder room.

I went overboard
double-billed my body that summer,
combining a mollusc allergy with tonsillitis
and my tonsils, nerf footballs
the size of acorn squash,
stonewalled me.

I fainted down the stairs to a basement
clinic near Restigouche.

Recovering in a boarding house
       —in New Brunswick?—
my dream of being choked
to death came to life.
I woke, sucking air, stealing air.

Vaillant

Our home was the third from the corner on a street directly across the Turcot Yards.

The perpetual groan of engines from the highways behind the traintracks were the roar were the ocean.

(Lay flat your ear against an autoroute hear the sea.)

Our view was unencumbered by housing developments. We had the openness of the railways and their surrounding lots full of wildflowers. Their wafting, wild sweetness pungent against the clouds of exhaust.

Up the hill, a car dealership guarded by two German shepherds whose larynxes had been surgically extracted. The dogs threw themselves against the chain fences, emitting urgent ghostly gasps whenever we walked past.

To the east, Saint Zotique's stone steeples cut into the sky. Across the way, the red brick block of the Toshiba factory, its lights burnt out in patches.

T S IBA.

Our first summer there, a prostitute lived on the corner, by the underpass. Men in their *bédaines* darted into her apartment at intervals. All through the night, between the rattling trains, the shifting of containers from truck to crane to train, I heard cars park and start up again.

Until her blood pooled on the sidewalk between our houses. My mother didn't believe me she'd been killed but then the cops showed up. It rained for a week, and the bloodstain in the broken sidewalk finally washed out.

In September, someone set the building on fire. Up Saint-Rémi was a Hells Angels bunker. Probably they did it. Maybe she was theirs.

But before all that, the girl sat in her low window on clear nights, fine brown hair down her back, right leg dangling from the frame, brushing the cement yard with her toes.

All sweat and lethargy.

And every night, as the stalling trains waited for their cargo, their motors thrummed a collective mechanical heartbeat that vibrated throughout our miniature house like an earthquake.

I never thought I'd get used to it.

In the middle of a dream I'd halfwake, holding the sides of my bed, the arrhythmic reverberations rocking me sound, close.

Cours du samedi

My mother stopped the car someplace in New Mexico.
Staunch miles of sunflowers chorused west
in unison. The poured-out sky
dripping all the way down the landscape

not just a line at the top
but filling all the space.

Zabriskie Point

My mother scraped her leg on a picnic table and the wound festered in Death Valley from the heat.

We'd been arguing about the two men who'd followed me, calling *Here, pussy, pussy,* their dog lolling out of the back of their pickup.

Where did you meet them, my mother asked, fixing her hair.

They followed me from the showers, I said, omitting my terror, washing halfdressed, worried they'd barge in; worse. As if a bit of pink cloth could stave them off, those two men and their dog, six hungry eyes. A bit of cloth and one eyehook lock.

The next morning we drove out to the desert. We stopped the truck. The motor ticked a while. A wake of footprints tamped out from a passing hare.

The rest was empty.

The Stare

"Come build in the empty house of the stare."
— Yeats

i.

We are each assigned a chair. One for Dad Bear, one for Mom Bear, one for K Bear, one for J Bear, and one for the cookie cutter blonde salvaged from the lost and found. Stank Bear. Fake Bear. Adopt-a-Bear.

ii.

Don't sit on the edge of the seat. This is not a music lesson. My chair is between the table and the cupboards. K Bear has a bread-covered chicken breast in the toaster oven. We are making chicken burgers. She squirts extra mayo on the buns. The buns are on the counter by the stove. This is the preparation area. This is my second supper. I'm getting fat. They feed me canned yellow beans. They feed me canned green beans. They feed me homemade bread. They say, *You have ruined our family.*

iii.

Rain. Rain falls daily rain falls every day. The smell of ferns and holly trickles into the family room, where I sleep. The gutter dribbles it in.

iv.

They tell me that I'm balding. They tell me I'm regressing. They tell me to watch *The Price Is Right* that's what that chair is for, for me to watch *The Price Is Right* with them as a Bear family. I hide under the sink of the downstairs bathroom and whisper into a cordless telephone, *I'm calling you from under the sink*. From the adjacent laundry room, my McDonald's uniform sloshes in the machine. The smell of fry oil doesn't wash out. From the adjacent laundry room, the smell of vinegar-soaked tiles.

v.

At night I vacuum straight lines along the turquoise carpet. So the house won't look lived in. So the house won't lose its value. I suction parallel trajectories along the wall-to-wall. One dark, one pale. One dark, one pale. One dark, one pale.

FLANKS SOUNDING HEAVILY WITH EXPIRATION

This is the dream: a horse crucified on a telephone pole stuck into orange desert dirt. The horse's wounds faucet red. A girl, twelve or thirteen, hair shiny charcoal (like a horse in a Colville), places herself between beast and cowboys. There are two cowboys upright in a kicked-open truck. Rifles cocked. There's a blue sky. A high arcing pale blue sky. Blue the colour of a carton of skim milk. One deepfried cartoon cloud. The horse's flanks stretch on the post, its breath bagging shallow girths of air.

Edisto

In the truck my roast pink mother floats in a piggy nightgown from the Piggly Wiggly. She's drinking piña coladas. I've got corn mash or some kind of corny bottled up nostalgia-moonshine tourist-trap rubbing alcohol. Gag. Bought our bottles at the package store across the marsh crawling with crabs big as silver dollars. Creeping marsh. Southern Birnam. At night we go to see the turtles spawn. My mother's bunioned footprints sidle turtlefin sandtracks. Underexposed whitecaps flick black and white and back. A centenarian loggerhead's eye beads. Dinosaur wan. Moon dandles a gelatinous turtle egg.

Rivière-du-Loup

The moon's a flat prop over the delta of the Saint Lawrence. The river opens here. Blue light hits the hills and fjords of the northern shore. Limonium salts the air. Waves suck out by Whisky Island, l'Île aux lièvres, l'Île verte.

Two crows on two dead trees. A dialogue of crows. The *caw caw caw caw caw* of crows. A third: *caw caw caw* to the other two. They sound off granite pebbles to the beaked jetty.

Mount Cannon by Way of
Lonesome Lake

We boulder over rocks swing our bodies from root to claw.
this still and murky lake, these planks on swamp
these very conifers
I watched them they watched me grow.

At the cloudy peak past the observation tower,
mosses fur the earth's cool crevices
visibility is mistdamp.
A ranger says, *You're the only two hikers I've seen today.*

We wind our way back to the car past
Echo Lake where my friend and I fought
over who would J-stroke,
along the bike path she and I tore up and down
on folding single-speeds,
past the brook we dammed to our knees.

I spent my childhood at this campsite.
It's just a campsite.
This ridge is home.

Here's where my mother taught me to build fires
pitch tents take coffee by the side of the road.
She taught me even steps to summit
never to run down a mountain.

We have named birds
we have shared with them our Shredded Wheat
we have locked eyes with apple-stealing coyotes
and it was a family of redhaired foxes
with guns and wifebeaters
who showed us how to boost the battery.

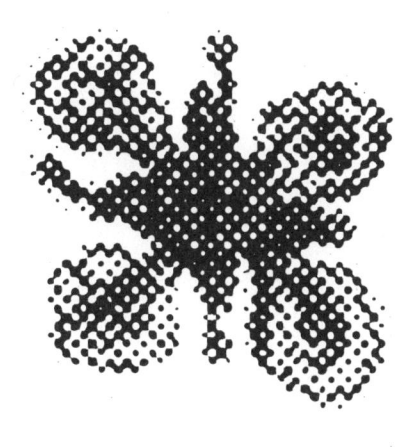

SKIRTING PETITE-PATRIE

Down with a Case of WTF

I bought some loose tobacco in some ye olde general store by the Harvard Yard. I had food poisoning and sat on the curb, trying not to shit myself, watching whitetrash ghetto Irish kids in bomber jackets appliquéd with Celtic insignia, schoolgirl women who bounced from campus in egalitarian Gap tweeds, shoulder-length hair parted to the side. One chubby Jackie O after another.

La Calera

i.

Stepping off too-tall sidewalks, near misses with cars, buses, donkeys. Breathless walking downhill.

Diego must renew his travel visa at the Canadian Embassy. We spend the day in lines that circuit beehive Nescafé highrises. A female soldier decked in fatigues and diamonds for each finger tells us she's been waiting since six-thirty that morning. Her hair's pulled taught in bleachedblonde cornrows.

> The dry Andes crowd this part of Bogotá, funneling wind between buildings. Tourists shiver in their summer getups.
> Palmeras grow short and stout as Boteros.

ii.

The waitress is nine and all business. *Pollo por el doctor*, who kicks stray dogs out from underfoot. *Agua de panela por la señorita*. The chicken on his fork, the rice, the beans, the gentleman behind him in a ruana, cigarette dangling from his mouth and another tucked behind his ear, shoes fresh shined, bowler hat askew. Dogs scatter, alternately barking at the arcing dirt road and at the shanties that around us crop. A woman carries her four-year-old in a fuzzy synthetic blanket with a picture of SpongeBob SquarePants. Cheese curds fatsmear my agua de panela. Fatsmear fatsmear fatsmear.

iii.

Echinacea thick in the air.

We painted our kitchen for you.

Gracias.

The maid nodding and asking about babies.

La esquela, I say, but she is nodding with her husband and rocking the air with her arms in encouragement.

Diego's mother saw a boy and a girl in her hot chocolate. Two babies. She will give us money. She will come to care for them and I can still go to school.

Better yet, she says I am smart enough already.

iv.

Paco is not the butler, Diego's parents explain. Paco is the gardener. They honk for him to come scurrying, obedient to *el doctor*. Paco lifts his baseball cap and laughs. Delight in service. Proud to unlock and open the gate. El doctor honks his appreciation—*bap bap-bap-bap-bap*—and drives the Volvo under the awning of the garage, beside the clamouring fuchsia hyacinth he says contain mild opiates. The stray dog bounds through the garden towards us. I'm not allowed to pet it in case of fleas. Paco the gardener runs uphill to finish dinner. He wears an ironed one-piece mechanic's suit and a Miami Marlins ballcap.

v.

Diego's mother pulls out a black lacquered guitar. *Guayabo negro pregúntale a la sabana si alguna vez por aquí me vio pasar.* Diego's teaching her new chords they're singing *guayabo negro maldito donde amarro mi caballo cuando llego del palmar.* I drink tinto with some guava dessert. Horses trot behind the ridge of echinacea trees at the far end of the property. Their hooves spatterclap like rain that's more sonorous than rain.

Nevsky Prospekt

A suited-up drunk careens off his steed, shouting at the sparsely moving traffic on the street. A young woman leads the horse by its bridle in high-hipped jeans, sneakers and blonde hair to her ass. Stray bitches lurch from fleets of streetcleaning Humvees, their halfdozen tits as rubbery as baby-bottle areolae. I walk past the McDonald's, past the Coca-Cola sign, past the restaurant with the guy decked out like a pirate all hours of the day. I don't know my address, but I recognize my place by the green Lada stranded in front of the building where in the courtyard, litters of kittens glom onto garbage containers, mewing and flicking their tails in the dusty beams of dawn's midmorning light. I unlock the twelve bolts on my door, shower under a dribble of rusty urine-stinking water in a fuchsia showerstall with a radio option and lay down between sheets printed with astrological signs on a plush pullout sofa. A dreamcatcher hangs from the ceiling fixture. When I take off my glasses it fuzzes out of focus and its plastic beads swing shapelessly in the breeze of the open window.

Neva

The boat moves through bloated canals in perpetual twilight. He's got a girl stuck like a burr to his shirt. We talk a little. His petulant intelligence reminds me of someone else. We clink bottles. A drawbridge strung up with lights breaks apart. We motor over wakes of jostling riverboats. A spray of white fireworks erupts from the embankment. I laugh, giddy from the extravagance of such staged beauty. We glide under a footbridge. I reach to slide my hand along a steel beam at its convex.

Scaffolding

i.

It was a beautiful night. The sky was so starry, so clear was the sky. There's a particular shape to the Québécois accent on the east end of the Plateau. It ducks into international French vowels, but the warmth of rural slang pushes out again in exclamations, belying region over education. It was a beautiful night, a night that we may only know when we are very young.

— *Bonjour.*
— *Ça va bien?*
— *Ouais, vous autres? Un croissant? Un panini?*
— *Un panini! T'ambitionnes.*

They are used to meeting at the same place and at the same hour. The man with the under-ambitious appetite carries a tall umbrella, closed. Charcoal suit. Wire glasses. Vapid face. Likely a lawyer. The permed blond with him is decked out in a polka-dotted, fishtailed dress and too much makeup. Neither are young. The waitress, pigeon-toed, thickening at the waist, asks about the woman's aunt:

— *C'est un changement dans sa vie. Elle a toujours vécu avec sa sœur. Est pas consciente d'où elle est. Moi comment j'm'appelle? 'E m'a dit, "J'ai une nièce qui s'appelle Lise mais c'est pas vous parce qu'elle elle a pas de lunettes."*

The man moves his seat to be next to the woman rather than across. He rests the back of his hand against the table and she takes it briefly. Sips her coffee. He's stretched out, legs splayed in front of him. She's proper. Calves crossed neatly at the ankles, the way the nuns taught her generation. Permanently poised for a photograph(er).

ii.

You thought for a second then took the seat beside me rather than across. The sky was so starry, so clear was the sky. I put my bag on the brick window-ledge. You drank vodka; I ordered brandy. Our waitress was about fifty, she was tired. She made signs for us to eat. We nodded our heads, *nyet*.

iii.

– *Qui vit dans l'édifice?*
– *Le Docteur Clown.*
– *L'architecte, aussi.*
– *L'association des lesbiennes.*
– *Ah, oui, l'architecte.*
– *Lui il reste.*
– *Les lesbiennes partent.*

iv.

A little distance away from the restaurant. You went to a convenience store to buy some cigarettes and a bottle of water. The lineup was long and the shop was cramped so I waited outside. An old babushka gesticulated with both her canes at my shoes, smiling in gummy encouragement.

I'd seen another like her the day before, dead on the sidewalk with a plastic bag barely covering her face, her hair the colour of nicotine stains, bushy and animated in the wind. A police officer stood watching traffic. Pedestrians milled around her like ants around a sandwich.

You came out and we crossed the street. We walked a little distance away from Nevsky. The air clogged up with sewage and dill. We rambled along the embankment, leaned against the guardrails, staring absorbedly at the murky canal waters. *What we need is another boat ride,* you said.

We wandered up and down the streets. Through a courtyard turned basketball court where a man walked a Rottweiler. I glanced over my shoulder at you as I balanced along the slim portion of sidewalk uncrowded by scaffolding. Your hand on my shoulder steering me under the scaffolding. So clear was the sky, that, looking at it, you could not help asking yourself: how can all sorts of cross and crotchety people live beneath a sky like this? A blue tarpaulin. The network of metal. My hat next to a puddle in the rectangle of the scaffolding's entry. That's a very youthful question, too.

v.

Chaotic mass at the cathedral, whose carillons shook out clanging time, ringing, discordant cowbells. A dozen riders galloped through traffic on miniature horses. I wandered up and down the streets in deep dejection, quite unable to understand what was the matter with me. I went to Nevsky Prospekt and I rambled along the embankment, and wherever I went I missed seeing the people I was used to meeting at the same place and at the same hour. *I missed you by about an hour, I think.*

vi.

A bruise, a tongue curling under it. *Any number of words better left unwritten.*

Recipe

Stow lees till gleams leech and crevices crook and clash. See the slim ratch stripe touch or blush or blotch. Strew streams and felt themes of promise and promise. Fear or ease. It's always the same. Stew them then flail them till qualm-simmered juices feud sticky and needy and near.

Callow and Rue

i.

They lean against the bar's window, their movements spooling in lapsed gestures. Her hand relays his fingers a smoked-down cigarette stub. Her eyes look used to hurt, sensitive to any current that might afflict.

>   (He leaves she and she to bleat.)

ii.

Her bike's in the living room. Her clean dishes stack on one side of the sink, his dirty pile's on the left (*vu de face*). A beaded purse hangs beside a bookcase, pricked through with pins. He makes me tea. Sets his stopwatch to time its steep. We talk on the porch. He wets a stale cigarette in his mouth, like a clarinet reed. When he reaches to light it I see a pitfull of hair

>   (puppet yawn with a yarnful of tongue).

His shoulders are narrow; his skin is darker than mine. Behind him: a yellow bookcase of aerosol cans, an iron, blue rubber gloves. Tied with string to the railings behind me: a bamboo divider he found on the street. My legs cross, red Chinese shoes hook into brick, bending my body into an embarrassment of figure-eights. Below, construction workers break holes into the sidewalk.

iii.

We reach around each other. My breasts flatten against his birdcage. His hand feathers my back. In the hall, he reports recent alien sightings in the southwest. I lean in for a punchline. A key picks the lock. Brass knobs screwturn from either side of the door. *Here's Rosemary for remembrance.* She tilt-a-whirls, redoubling for a paystub with the greatest unease

while static flaps
through the spilt air milkweed.

Near Miss

Rode up leaflittered Clark
traces of hand underskirt
sober in spite of the beers on his tab
and the giddy moonclear streets
back sticky as his jaegerbreath call,
Who're you fucking?

Unsheafed
unleavened umbilicus shrimp.
Who're you fucking?
Clotsticky as dawnbreath
I was a card.

Neuter

Hell is a roomful of pregnant women staring at me with fakedout joyful empathy as I wait to get my tumour checkedup. Got the Bukowski. Got the Bukowski and the paper but the paper's all full of Michael Jackson and there's a little rajah boy bawling pulling his stroller over patient feet who knock back grins of forced tenderness while his tented mothers flock. Old man grinning grabbing vapidly at the babies generally like he has some memory of progeny he enjoyed.

Hello hello hello say hi say hi.

His wife is immobile beside him skin like wax. Baby the baby's crying until he can get his stroller and these rows and rows of breeding women with shirts dangling over pants gowns dangling over legs centres of gravity leavened leavening bellies commas and parenthesizing. Must I must I really be expected to hand it all over to the queasy squealing rage of wants must I continue to clean as if this dream were something sweet as if I were expected to get in on this dream. Husbands looking at me in my short dress sitting unpaired with my paperback and my paper and my scowl askance and exasperated these children's demeaning faces and their contorted women waddling sluggish halfsmiling as if they must display a natural fondness for breeding. One's chalked out exhausted bandaid beige her face fleshy bovine fingers used to milking used to working until elbows sterile.

In comes doctor. Yeah yeah of course act natural make a V.

Did it get bigger.

It's not for you to see, says the nurse cranking the condomed k-y camera deeper.

Beautiful, says doctor. *You have a beautiful uterus,* he says, *and you can wipe yourself off on your gown.*

Door swings hallway sounds sound in. Machine whirs whirs whirs. In the halfdark room the gibbous moon of my cyst glows from the screen like a miracle like a golfball. My own homemade parthenogenesis project.

Hello hello hello say hi say hi.

XX-XY = O.

JEAN-TALON

Saw him at the market
bundled in electric blue
sausage sandwich wrapped in tinfoil
cigarette.
Leaves debrised mosaic underfoot
underwheel
cauliflower deals applecarts beasts roasting on spits
to the tune of three for one
drum ukulele panpipe.
He said, *Nice glasses.*

Pushkin eggs regret
loaded up my bicycle basket southwards down Saint-Laurent.
Last spring his limbs bent on a folding chair
heron in the Green Room
I shot him down.

Dante

In August I sat in a yellow dress
on that bench banked under snow
pulling fortunes from cookies
from the Tonkinois resto
over there.

    Listen not to vain word or empty tongue.

February and we're cutting
through he's lifting me up in iconic
wooing posture we're like a pair of groping
figureskaters in galoshes.
The bench half-buried
my hands burrowed.

Everett

Words prune. We parse a spare
courtship. He says it was in the hallway
in front of the elevators.

I remember. He had his trousers rolled.
*It's been a long time
coming,* he says.

I grow bold.

D'ICI

His lanky figure's framed
à contre-jour.

Smoke and snowy air
ribbon in.

I drink in the easy sight,
Milk, no sugar.

Arc

Plastic strips sluice up and down December beams
string against the white apartment
the mismatched chairs the buckwheat pancakes
while blinds stripe light
on white and whiter white.

It is too cold for snow.
The day's low sun feeds pale
slights through blinds in ribbons stripes
the cold apartment the mismatched chairs.

To lie along the floor and warm
with pairs or plaited lights
to colour pairs to dapple cooler white
to curl against the strikes of light
that feeble fade and dusk.
To curl against the stripes of light
till we are grey with dusk and night.

Tithes

i.

My students in their polyester suits
half-slipping off their shoulders
and their breasts
countdown retirement in English—

thirty-seven years
seventeen years—

chorus the mendacity of quotidian commutes
West Island buses
weekend where *not-*
ing ap-
pen.

Nothing happens.

ii.

They like me here.
Smiles from the waitresses
compliments on my fur hat.

Barely enough money for dogfood
I changed my last twenty
got a croissant, an *allongé*.

A whitesmocked kitchengirl
carries loaves overhead.
A man in paintsmattered clothes says to a blonde
half his age,
You must speak German.
She says she's Norwegian.

Snow pinpricks
catch the sloping cubist
beams on the other side of the window.

Valentine

She lets me sleep in. I'm grateful. I put on my moccasins, go into the kitchen. Turn up the heat. Peer at the garbage. There's enough room. I dump out the grinds from the percolator, they make a thunk. The damp little circle could be pretty, if it wasn't for the smell of organic cow rotting in the hanging plastic bag. I rinse the pot out, just barely. No one will care about aluminium mushrooms. Put in some coffee, turn the element of the stove on to high. My dog's sleeping on the floor. I pour her a bowl of dogfood. I say, *Look, pellets!* She raises one eyebrow, then the other, but doesn't move. I pull out my favourite saucepan—the beige one from Village des Valeurs. It's got '70s style caricature flowers on its side. Pour in some milk. Whole milk. Stir a bit. Get my toast. Rye bread is best. Slide a pair of slices into the toaster. I pull out a record, something nostalgic, like from before anyone became Yusuf anything. Get my seven-dollar Ile d'Orléans blueberry jam out of the fridge, got my butter all loosey goosey melty on the table already, my prune yoghurt. I put my grandmother's plate on my mother's *canadienne* pine table and pour the almost burnt coffee into my mug. I spread out my books around me. The one about libraries, the old *Atlantic* with all the writers, the journals. The butter melts on the toast and the jam warms into the butter. The coffee's too hot but the milk didn't skin. I pick up the library book and smear jam in the margin and spill crumbs in the spine. I think about Virginia Woolf and her gossipy intelligence and I look through the plastic-covered patio windows to my backyard, where snow's piled waist deep, reflecting the late morning's bright cold. My dog dreams dog dreams.

Game

i.

Twenty bucks of pitchers.
My face maps laugh tracks
over a couple of side streets.
He cocks his head—*That's where I live.*

He settles behind me on the sofa debating
yes no yes and revelations
of a relay race for me he'd lost.
Don't go. We can just sleep.
Gets out shorts and a T-shirt. Keep my underpants
on. The fuchsia
pair. We spoon like old hands.

Morning alarms
pin. Chuck the mop out of the tub
to shower. They never have soap. He watches me
dress from the bedroom doorframe
narrating something.

Taxi to the university.
Deliver a speech. On a Saturday
hungover. There's no coffee.
In the front row another forced friendship takes rote.
I sweat through yesterday's clothes.

ii.

Note the way his grin
abashed and sweet
belies his disappointments.
Or mine. Our features shoot off blanks
for sport.
I skim for looks I've read before.

The Lark

Mornings
starlings parliament the dogpark.
Bright as their goldflecked wingblades
love shrugs into a secondhand coat
where our two hands crowd a pocket.

Pigeontoed lilt from the metro
peck a peck a peck goodbye
see his saunter flock footprints
past the lineup of cabs
lisp of brown curl a comma against his slim neck. I'd say
chestnut.

Everything is budding.
We mynamimic with fists
that spring open to close and anastosmose
until thumb and index cocked we aim
for the bullseye in a duel where we win
bullets whistling through alleys like clothespegs
the cocksure snap of mettle
and we die a couple of times.
Maybe three or four.

Four Eyes

Ice cream sandwiches,
paper-bagged Pabst,
nicotine distress.

He meets me on the street
in some red sweatshirt red jeans getup
and *the most comfortable shoes!*
from the second hand store.

He grabs me and says
I'm his best friend. Suspect
given his discomfort.

We lie back
egg on the sky over Parc Jarry.

His fickle determination
follows me: agog, critical.
He comments on a zit,
on the lowness of my brow,
my *cheerleader thighs.*

He scopes a girl in royal blue
strung up in a camera necklace.
Two boys wait for her idyll.
A trio of gawky deer,
by the bulrushes.
A tableau you could Instagram.

It's true I ate a fishburger trio for breakfast.
My McDonald's sickness now indistinguishable
from the nauseating thought of loss.

Plaza Saint-Hubert Reconciliation Number Double-Digit

Headless mannequins pivot from their heels and bump into each other in clumsy slowmotion. Pigeonshit crusts the sidewalks. The odd passerbyer surprised to scope our makeout spot. We're on a park bench between a discount houseware shop and a store full of 1950s child mannequins gussied up in satin first communion wear.

One of the baby mannequins is black, the others are oh-so-precious white in white.

Draft

That spring I felt hope *à fleur de peau*.

A warm breeze. The smell of green. Dear.

And the crush.

I wrote about him: *Our days float like yesterday's cottonwood spores in that perfect blue sky.*

Fluff.

Radii

platonic / platinum

I could lick the hair of his arms to
smell the sunlight
but let the lilac air
wheel-speak our sympathies.

Late evening slanting through halfclosed lids.

bespoke / besotted

This morning I cut
through the baseball diamond.
I found a fractured robin's egg

iris blue.

Call Me Klaus

i.

Boy circa 1952—
all cheekbones.
Tongue curled up in concentration
slice of navel
tastes like cigarettes.

ii.

Hands hold the bedframe.
He curls into my armpit.

How would you spell fistfight?

Feet touching feet.
A hand outlines my torso.

iii.

He comes in from a cigarette
on my balcony. The other night
there was a skunk in the neighbour's yard
by the catalpa tree.
Maybe he saw it
digging up the yard.

Flush

Squatting Cabot Square
cracking pastel pralines into paper cups
night globes over the old pissoir.
We're killing time before the movie starts.

Mohawks
punks
men chucking canes drag their heels their mini hounds
lag on leashes we shuffle conversation

a rough hand shades a smoke.
We're not that nervous.
We say some things.

Wont

At a café full of up-and-coming Mexicans, we drank Coca-Colas out of glass bottles. Lips fit snug on rims, a pleasing kind of bottle BJ. Beside me, a girl pretty despite her acne. Beside Yann, her boyfriend. Boy-boy, girl-girl—like that.

The boy wore cutoffs and black Converse hightops. He had a small tear in his shirt, by the cuff of his sleeve. I thought he probably didn't have health care. Maybe her either. Imagine the debt they'd be in if they got into an accident.

> *Don't worry about getting shot—that was a stupid, overprotective thing for me to mention.*

She wore a flowered blouse. He was on his computer. She wrote in a notebook. How could they live there and drink coffee and not freak out.

> *inviting you to get some coffee was actually the first thing i thought of when i got your email, but then, you know, that's all kinda complicated.*

It was a warm night.

This is what Yann's face looks like: there is a line drawn from his cheekbones to his jaw that bends his gold-specked cheeks into three dimensions. Even teeth. Skin reveals more freckles, if you look at him when light is hitting his face directly.

That morning we'd walked through an underpass where at the end of the tunnel a feral parrot blinked down from its perch on a barbed wire fence. Emerald head cockatoo. Yann said maybe it's carrying messages. I thought he said maybe it's carrying Mexicans.

> *A Quaker parrot,* you wrote. *They're wild here.*

Once I dreamed you mailed me your first novel. It had the same cover as X. (I saw it there, second to bottom shelf, parallel to the cash register.) In my dream the last line of the book was *So I married the teacher,* which was basically a waste of a dream. In my dream you showed up at my house with a bucket of plums. I dreamed that a few years ago.

> *does it feel longer or shorter than a year since i met you? it depends on the time of day, i think.*

When I lived at my old place. The summer I had the miscarriage and told people I had tonsillitis. (The work bathroom. A garbage can. The surprise. I didn't even know.) My roommate let me listen to some downloaded Joan Didion on her laptop. The computer on a pillow by my head.

For a couple days I lay there hazing in and out of sleep and grief and felt the loss of things I wasn't wont to crave accrue.

Ruse

i.

I was out with this guy
who asked me to name the happiest day of my life.

We were eating a five-course meal.
I was wearing a backless T-shirt and a fuchsia
skirt that came with the apartment.
Or we were at his place by Parc Jeanne-Mance
watching *Blood Diamond* on his laptop.

I thought the question showed a lack of depth.
His answer was at the ready: an overeager
account of a commune and a struggle through surf
to plant a handsewn flag adorned with an icon
of a new earth, or a peace
sign. And even though he'd chased
me after our second date and we hadn't kissed to kiss me
by a fire escape I considered maybe he was a bad idea overall
and I didn't have a best day of my life to share.

ii.

Those few seconds.
Your face reflected—
and thirty other thoughts competed for your features.

Later you said, *Your eyebrows did this thing.*
I didn't tell you I was on the pill
and I thought about how Father Ryan told me he got hep
from a transfusion but I never believed him. I thought he got hep from
sex and I could too. I said, thinking of a poem
by Robin Becker, *It can be good to want*
and you said, *It can be good to have.* Stressing
have.

It was all the beats leading up to
my *eyebrows doing this thing*
and you downstairs telling me your last name
tearing half a page from your notebook
and writing your email in allcaps
saying, *Is this it. Will I never see you again.*
Your voice pitching up.
I watched you walk, hands in your hoodie,
lights pooling you in and out of dark puddles.

I went to sleep.
You wear pyjamas, you'd said.
Or, *those are real pyjamas.* They were my mom's.
They had heart
buttons, or daisy buttons,
and I didn't know if you liked real
pyjamas or if you thought they were stupid.
I woke up because my boyfriend was calling from overseas
and I knew it had passed

but I didn't know how waiting would gape
me open. Waiting's eyebrows possibly *doing this thing*
as it chewed over it remembering.
Waiting being on the rag.
(*Of course you're on your period.*)
Waiting waiting for an explanation about how Xanax
eased you after cheating
kind of a performance piece that sucked.
Waiting hurt when you said, *You're sweet you like to cuddle.*
I don't know why; nerves.
If it could be carbonated
waiting going up my nose.

You said, *I never saw grey eyes before.*
and something about blondes with moles on their shoulders.
The subject had been discussed with a friend who also cheated
and you'd agreed we were a covetable type.

The kind you don't write to
just write back
because that's not cheating.

That Line

And then that sentence popping out at me at a café. I felt like I'd gotten caught. I was sitting by a window. It was raining. I looked out at Mile End. People like wet cats. Like if you said cats to mean hipsters. Like if you halfsang it in a musical—*Mari-aa*. Some puddles. The patchouli hub of the café.

It wouldn't have mattered which one I'd picked.

Not a Good Time

You say, *Don't be nervous.* Your expression when you say that is the same as last summer. Sort of the same. Not really. You're less intent. Your eyebrows don't quote your eyes the way they can.

(We walked by Wilensky's. I remembered when I felt so bold as to say, *If ever you come to Montreal—*)

The light in the white room on the grey sofa on the white chair. The bed. Blankets folded back on the left. I want to want it. I imagine tucking myself under the opened covers. A nap. A week. A month. A day.

You sit on a chair. I sit on a chair. There's a bay window and a park out the window. Your thumb is stained from smoking. The skin of your thumb is peeling. You look worn out. You say if we'd fucked six years ago we'd still be fucking now. You say, *We have an arrangement.* You say the great thing about anal is how you can watch the pussy and still be fucking.

You should have come before today. Minus the ebullience we are electric with discomfort. It feels so off I laugh. I think people in the hall can hear me.

ELOQUENT AREAS

Fuse

for Frederik

I peony
flex
till rot
gape
wilting weight.

I copse in decay's direction.
Bloom bloom's bursts.
Swoon
till seed.

Weather

Do all daddy's girls pit their Pas
against Prospero? They'd have to be anglos,
squareheads, colonized expats,
or part of the Commonwealth.

They'd have to be classically
versed. The type whose fathers read
them Shakespeare. Cervantes. Spyri. The Bible.

They'd have to be brainchildren
invented versus begotten
daughters to be handed
to an entitled suitor. They'd have talked
about a bookish man. A navy man.
A man with a craft.

A man like Prospero.
Only prosperous, less metaphysical,
less wasted, less.

What three things
if you were shipwrecked?

Daddy deliberates between himself
and the mariner (and nothing).

Daddy wants the mariner because
even though he didn't have to chop the wood
he did.

The rapt servitude
of a daughter
without the gift to spell

a word—
island.

Two Pears

The first poem I sent him about himself.
It was a postcard. From Vancouver.
Probably bought at the art gallery.

Two pears, with crumbling cheese.
The sounds of the CBC
Peach tea

I don't remember the rest. I was thinking of a day after high school. In January or February. His girlfriend was gone maybe singing a dirge. We could be freer without her monitoring the exchange of our love. (*You're fucking each other,* she said. *You have to understand how sick she is,* he said.) I sat on the counter I'd have to Javex-clean that night. Peter Gzowski on the radio. A pre-night-shift 4 PM ease. Fragrant peach tea. A block of very old cheddar. He ate his raisins on the side, cupped them into his dirty hands, grabbed them out of their plastic bag with his dirty fingernails and tossed them back into his mouthful of yellow teeth ungraciously and glad.

(Remember: a bowl of walnuts on Hampton Street, the mystery of a nutcracker not in the shape of ballerina boy in Christmas garb.)

The Heart of an Ox

Abigail's heart is pierced by two centrifugal pumps

if you place a stethoscope
to her ribcage you won't hear a pulse.

A girl with matching pink

—they weren't fuchsia—

the sound of her flip-flop steps
flutter behind me uphill.

My landmarks are forgotten faces and I've dreamed
these buildings, this skyline
not remembering they were here.

I lost my virginity in one of these dorms—

got waylaid. Haha. Get it.

I caught a ride
with an engineering student who drove a black sports car.
He taught me the word *subwoofer*.

A chocolate bar melted in the top
pocket of my blue canvas backpack.

I went back to my place.
Back to babysitting.
How under-ambitious I must have seemed.
The teenager no one wanted
to adopt squatting a trailer in someone's driveway
dropped out of community college
never overly athletic.

He preferred another girl
who sort of looked
like me but was better than me at everything.

I sent my father the NPR article
about Abigail, the cow,
and her heart, about a year
or two after his heart surgery.

(But before the NPR piece on how we can hack
into people's heart devices
—picture it—bombing a dictator
    from the inside.)

We talked: *imagine no heartbeat.*

Mrs. Woods, my Sunday school
teacher, had a pacemaker that ticked
louder than her windup Timex.

The first thing my dad did when he woke

—with a start—

from surgery was to talk conservative
plots to fund terrorism. He knew his nurse
from the drop-in centre at church.

I know her from the drop-in
centre, he said.
I didn't feel any pain
but I could hear them
playing heavy metal.

To pass the hours of his operation
I'd been reading a girl I didn't know
then was my husband's ex.
I didn't know I'd have a husband, didn't know
her boyfriend would be it

      (she looks a little like him
      and she's better than me at everything).

The last time I had time to walk
around a strange city alone like this was when I met you

      (I didn't know until I was in Germany.

      I tell myself you don't think of me.
      I think you can tickertape like that better than I can).

The last time I saw a movie in Vancouver it was *The English Patient*. I thought, let me have this

    (melodrama).

The line from *The English Patient* I recited to myself—
    Every night I cut my heart out
    but in the morning it was full again.

Tonight I saw a movie where a couple argues,
no holds barred, the way we do,
and then laces themselves
tentatively back together again, the way we do.

    Every night I cut my heart out—

No pulse, still running.

The Grief Marathon

I want to slurp scotch from a cereal
bowl, snack on hash cookies iced
with Ativan. I want to sprawl
in bed laptop cracked ninety-five degrees

Say Yes to the Dress
on one tab, gonzo porn on another.
I want bags spilling American Apparel duds
their uncut tags dangling showy
as Christmas tree ornaments.

I want fresh tattoos on every knuckle
and pain with every bend of my hand.
AS. IF.
I could numb myself
into becoming a lost boy (I never was).

Out the window
the maple's branches scratch the balcony
railings. A palm I left out all summer browns,
dusts.

Last year
my father and I sat out back
watched a posse of tomcats slink
down the alley in single file.

I said, *Remember the time all those cats
showed up in my bedroom?*
He said he did.

I remembered how he kept his wedding
band on his bureau a good three
months before he pawned it.

Now

Now! he shouts, *Now! Now! Now! Now!*
He's stuck on the toilet.
The orderly has to get another man to help lift
him. His legs are withered sticks
narrow as his grandfather's shillelagh
he's still dead weight.

Oh my oh my oh my I can't stop saying oh my.
He says they're hitting him.
I stroke his neck. His back.
He shouts, *Oh Oh* and his defibrillator leaps

bubble gum bubbling his skin popping his heart
more than once. More than twice.

First instinct is to step back
but I hug him tight. Every shock pains
him. We ease him back into bed. He turns to his side
and cradles the railing. *I thought that was it,*
he says. So did I.

(His fingernails are full of shit.
Do you know your father plays with his feces now? They said.
No.
*Will your father commit double-suicide with his married
Calgary ladyfriend?* They ask.
Probably not.)

A nurse with dangling ornament earrings says,
T'as l'air tannant, fake flirting, fake encouraging.
He likes pretty girls. It works, a little.

I unwrap his Christmas presents
tuck them into the plastic dresser on wheels
by the closet of unused clothes.

There is a card on the dresser from his ex
that says *Goodbye* beside a bag of broken
peanutbutter cookies she baked
for this occasion.

BATTERMEDOWN!

Grief compression.
A spaceship garbage disposal
boiling down the grist.
A greasy garbage soup
we slosh and slosh and slosh.

Any memory of love evaporates.
And this watery consommé chafes.
Chafes. Blisters. Dries and grinds grief
grief pulverizes.

There is an all-caps refrain. It goes:

LIFE IS NOT AS IDLE ORE
BUT IRON DUG FROM CENTRAL GLOOM
AND HEATED HOT WITH BURNING FEARS
AND DIPPED IN BATHS OF HISSING TEARS
AND BATTERED WITH THE SHOCKS OF DOOM

It goes:

TO SHAPE
AND USE
BATTERMYHEART THREEPERSON'DGOD
TO SHAPE
AND USE

It goes:

FOR YOU AS YET BUT KNOCK, BREATHE, SHINE, AND
SEEK TO MEND—

ARISEANDFLYTHEWHEELINGFAUNTHESENSUAL-
BEASTMOVEUPWARDWORKINGOUTTHEBEAST

It goes:

    Life is not as idle ore but iron dug from central gloom and heated hot with burning fears and dipped in baths of hissing fears and battered with the shocks of doom to shape and use.

Batter my heart, three-person'd God; for you as yet but knock,
breathe, shine, and seek to mend.
Batter me down, three-person'd god
arise the wheeling faun the sensual hiss
to smack and doom
to ape to tiger die.

To shape and use. To shape and use. To shape and use. To
shape and use. To shape and use.

Mourning?

or mindlessness sloppy agitation
breathing four slow breaths won't help I want
to tether myself to a stern and rigorous
religion stop the steps just act them
out until my end or revelations turn me
I become a witness to the miracle of my salvation
I wasn't crazy I was just becoming a better person.

> (There is no reason to hate my given name. It's a pretty name I
> don't know why I've thought it was too soft and trendy.)

Bind myself to revelations a masthead a prow the *stjerne* this star this star this star.

1:00 - 2:00 PM Décarie and Paré

How many Tim Horton's bagels with butter and Swiss and a medium hot chocolate on the highway. I've hated my life for two years but I can't tell if that's job-related or life-related or my dad being a shit and then dying-related or maybe I need medication in a more daily way to make the Décarie and the fake bagel and the sexy video descriptions more palatable and get my gratitude on I'm so grateful to have a writing job I'm so grateful to have a study full of Ikea furniture I'm so grateful to have won a 40" TV I'm grateful for this Target outfit I'm grateful for this sterling silver ring I'm grateful for this coral lipstick made in Montreal.

Playboy Cybergirl Shallana Marie poses with her surfboard in a slick black one-piece bathing suit that leaves very little to the imagination. Let's be frank a moment. Did you ever see such a plunging one-piece? Probably not. Not in real life.

I didn't want to go to the spa and every morning I clean the house and the cat puked three more times and even over my dad's really nice red woven wool blanket and all I can picture is getting a hotel room for myself and watching some big, anonymous TV. I'd sleep at the Ruby Foos, by work, by the autoroute.

There are just these two little black straps, like suspenders, that run down Shallana Marie's curvaceous torso. It's the kind of bathing suit you have to be very careful not to displace. Unless you're in San Tropez, possibly, where that kind of top part of your bathing suit displacement is perfectly natural.

Red light. I kick at a bank of ice with my black rubber boots. Kicking at a block of ice on a street corner is childish. It's 2:00 PM I have to be back at the porn bunker to edit the video descriptions now. And then I'll go visit my father at the home. It smells like shit and juice there and there's the wheelchair lady who hangs in the doorway threshold she grinds her teeth goes, *Ahhhh! Ahhh! Ahh!* in a frightening warblescream and the guy with one eye who wears a fannypack around his neck and pulls out coins the Knights of Columbus left him for Christmas to show me and the guy I call Boss (*Salut Boss*) who paces up and down the hallway twelve hours a day who used to go up and down the isles of his brother's thread factory in Victoriaville to check no one was smoking because the whole place would go up like a tinderbox if someone even lit a match. I probably won't be able to stomach going to the party after. Maybe I should cancel on my friends tomorrow, too. Better to just be quiet than to see anyone and risk freaking out in public, like I did last summer, at the restaurant, and then cried down Saint-Denis all the way home.

To most of us red-blooded Americans that dramatic, plunging V remains a welcome jolt to the system, though, and that's not a bad thing. We're all for welcome jolts.

All of my friends must know I'm depressed because I'm depressing to talk to. I cross the autoroute. It's minus twenty-five I picture the picture of where I'd cut my wrists. By the canal. Wrapped in blankets. I picture jumping off the bridge. I picture getting an IUD, a *sterilet*, so I wouldn't have to burden any children with my depression. Or what if I totally nutout after postpartum and I never come back. How long have I been depressed? Two years? All along? Just since he's been sick? Was it all depression? A sane reaction to a Dickensian childhood. What does it feel like to be people. I'm just trying it all on. Job and matching house things and longer hair and makeup everyday and knowing what kinds of weddingrings Edwardian or Victorian or Tiffany's setting or modern and holiday roastbeef and not looking like you try too hard. Don't want to be foolish. Don't want to have missed it. Have to learn how to do it right.

(What we'll do is we'll keep his ashes in the closet or in the storage space until the funeral. And then I'll have to take the box I ordered and throw the ashes into Georgian Bay at some point. He said, *I don't want to be buried in Quebec! Don't bury me in Quebec.* I said okay. I'll take him to his parents' cottage. His dad died there but he was buried in Toronto.)

The narrative: Shallana Marie practices surfing. She then slips her fine self into the water because she's just so hot she really should cool down. It's really a health matter. And she's doing the right thing for her health and safety, and ours, too. Suddenly, goddess-like she emerges. Water runs in rivulets over her tanned body.

I shouldn't have called him. I'm always breaking everything and everyone wants to say I'm always breaking everything.

That sounds crazy persecution complex mania dirty backwater whispervoice but it's true. There are many actual individual stories to back that up. Like with my halfsister, when she went to my dad's church and gave him some poinsettias and said I'd ruined the family. I dreamed last night that I made her apologize for that. She did, in the dream. This Christmas my mother gave me a bottle of iced apple cider from her and she said your sister's there for you. All the years I called her for her birthday and for Christmas and she never called me. I ran into her in the street once after she'd gotten a facial and she said *Do I look too granola like this—with no makeup on?* As if we'd just hung out, as if we knew each other and the last time I saw her wasn't a decade before. It took them seven years to notice I wasn't attending Christmas dinners and now it's all, *Oh she has problems she doesn't even like Christmas.*

My brokenness is giving leeway as I age. The gap widens and widens in my wake. The only thing that works to bandaid the sight of it is pop tunes and romance novels and crime TV. Banal makes me feel okay. Shrinks my goals. Cozies around me. Wraps a buoying berth. Tight, tight, deep-tissue tight.

Here we must take a moment. We really have to pause and possibly get out our gratitude journals: the perfection of Shallana Marie's booty is really undeniable.

Sainte-Catherine

I had a dream you told me, *What was I supposed to do.* Our family was going to Iceland and I was trying to make them go to Mexico instead. I said, *Let me see your wedding ring* and you sighed and showed it to me. I showed you mine. You asked me what our combined income was.

I dreamed I was shopping at Marimekko, which was a tiny store on Sainte-Catherine. You could also buy Finnish meals there. I chose the tuna. It was a tuna salad and they cracked an egg and poured the egg yolk into the salad and it started to cook. My father was there. I said, *There will be a lot of protein in this.*

There was a cottage before and something about someone being afraid they'd had hurt her daughter by not teaching her to drive. They gave me a vial of salt water. I poured it over each eye to soothe them.

There was a beach.

I was in jail.

I was in a jailbus.

I was with people who unknowingly ate a lot of goldflakes.

In the mountains. In BC. It made them drunk.

I made my father a bed and then he said, *Oh, I shat myself.*

These

i.

An insect trapped in a web of electrodes. Catheters. Bed propped halfway up. Ten o'clock August morning light streaming into the ICU windows. A view to a courtyard. The irregular digital monitoring signals. Oxygen pumping in and out. Barrel chest inflating and collapsing with each compression of the oxygen pump.

ii.

Learning to read in the upstairs living room (when my parents lived together). The Q-cards on the floor with my father's cramped letters: *Samia is in the kitchen.* Sunbeams. Dust motes. My puppet Trump (Trunk + Trompe = Trump)—a camel.

iii.

Cinderella at the Snowdon Theatre. An ice storm. Hampton Avenue silver glass-coated. My father's centre of balance in his belly. He slips. I haul him back up. My shoulder a cane.

iv.

We practice dialing on the rotary phone.

Home is 483-2343
Work is 849-6154

v.

The transistor radio in the kitchen. Peter Gzowski.
The one o'clock count.

vi.

I spent my whole life looking for God outside but he is here! He points with his good hand to the coppery cumulus the golden swarming over his chest. *I see it,* I say.

vii.

His eye unshuts meets mine. Watery and present as a whale's.

ACKNOWLEDGEMENTS

To my parents, Rob Bull and Suzanne Blouin, thank you for your love, for the rigour of your aesthetics, for your engaged, contagious curiosity.

Thank you, Pascale Rafie, for egging me on with your talent and propping me up with your big sisterly encouragement.

Thank you team Soulgazers—Anna Leventhal, Sean Michaels and Jeff Miller—for being such a killer writing group.

Lasse Mathiesen Køhlert, my talented brother-in-law, thank you so much for the beautiful cover.

Mike Spry, Jessica Howarth, Ann Ward, Elee Kralji Gardiner, Drew Nelles, Ian Sullivan Cant, Shanti Maharaj, Melissa Thompson, Emma Healey, and Haley Cullingham, thank you so much for the close reads you've given any project I've thrown your way.

Thanks to Susan Musgrave, Sina Queyras, Mikhail Iossel, Rachel Rose, Gail Scott, Carmine Starnino, David McGimpsey, Suzanne Hancock, and Mary Di Michele for your ready encouragement and advice over the years.

Thank you to everyone at Anvil, in particular Brian Kaufman and Shazia Hafiz Ramji, for your suggestions and edits.

And thanks especially to my supersmart partner, Frederik Byrn Køhlert, for sharing this ramshackle, book-filled home with me and the SpiseMusKat. ("For love...makes one little room an everywhere.")

ABOUT THE AUTHOR

Melissa Bull is a Montreal-based writer, editor and translator. She is the editor of *Maisonneuve* magazine's "Writing from Quebec" column and her work has appeared in such publications as *Prism, Event, Playboy, Urbania, Broken Pencil* and *Lemon Hound*. Her translation of Nelly Arcan's collection, *Burqa of Skin*, was published by Anvil Press in 2014. *Rue* is her first collection of poetry.